The Day it Rained Chocolate Milk!

by Stacy Spriggs
August 6, 2011

Illustrations by Michael Edison
and Albert Adam Lichi

AuthorHouse™ LLC
1663 Liberty Drive
Bloomington, IN 47403
www.authorhouse.com
Phone: 1-800-839-8640

Published by AuthorHouse 08/05/2013

ISBN: 978-1-4678-7028-3 (sc)
*   978-1-4918-0840-5 (e)*

Library of Congress Control Number: 2013909287

Any people depicted in stock imagery provided by Thinkstock are models,
and such images are being used for illustrative purposes only.
Certain stock imagery © Thinkstock.

This book is printed on acid-free paper.

Because of the dynamic nature of the Internet, any web addresses or links contained in this book may have changed
since publication and may no longer be valid. The views expressed in this work are solely those of the author and do not
necessarily reflect the views of the publisher, and the publisher hereby disclaims any responsibility for them.

authorHOUSE®

This book is dedicated to my children (Alan, Joshua, and Sierra) for keeping my heart young. They are passionate about drinking chocolate milk every day, and would surely enjoy an endless supply. This book is also dedicated to my best friend, Holly, for her everlasting support.

It was a hot summer day. But, it was a day like any other day. We were playing on our fort, and wishing we had something else to do. We had already played super-heroes three times and hide-and-seek. I had a new bruise from falling off my bike and my sister was mad because I didn't want to have another tea party. The sky was getting darker.

Suddenly, out of nowhere, came a huge black cloud. The wind was blowing leaves all around us. I thought this would be a good chance to try out my new dragon kite. But, then Mom called for us to come inside since it was thundering.

"Well no kite for me," I thought. I said to my sister, "Come on, let's go inside and do a puzzle." Before we could get inside the door, it began to rain. But, it did <u>not</u> look like rain water – it was brown. It didn't smell like rain either. It smelled sweeter, like cake or candy.

My sister looked a little scared. She asked, "What is it?" Well, I didn't know what to say, so I licked my arm and told her, "It tastes like chocolate milk!" We couldn't believe it!

Then, I knew exactly what I needed to do. I ran inside and grabbed some buckets and pots. I set them out all over the yard so they would catch some of the milk. They started filling up fast. I thought this must be the best day of all time!

By now, my sister wasn't scared at all anymore. She was splashing in chocolate milk puddles. She was really dirty! We both tried to catch it with our tongues. Mom was just staring at us and shaking her head like she couldn't believe her eyes.

We ran to the front yard because Dad was just getting home from work. The windshield wipers were smearing the chocolate milk, so he could barely see to drive. He was soaked from driving with the windows down. He said, "Come on guys, let's go for a walk!"

We grabbed our umbrellas and started walking toward the neighborhood pool. Everything was coated with brown liquid. The air smelled so good and chocolaty. It didn't feel very good when it dripped in your eyes, but it sure tasted yummy. Dad kept saying how this had never happened before in ALL the history of time and it must be some kind of weather mix-up. I said, "Maybe some chocolate factory had an explosion."

While we were walking, I noticed a fire hydrant and wondered if there was chocolate milk inside of it, too. I asked Dad if chocolate milk could put out a fire. He said it would probably depend on what was burning and how big the fire was. My sister was making up a silly song about messy giants in the clouds spilling their cups.

When we got to the pool, there were kids swimming in chocolate milk!! They were having lots of fun jumping and splashing around in it, but no one could see where they were going when they tried to swim underwater. Some boys were squirting each other with water guns, and there was a girl pretending to be a mermaid lost in the mud.

The milk was flowing down the street and into grates. Then, pipes took it underground to lakes. Here in Florida, all of those lakes eventually connect to the ocean. Dad was saying that it may not be healthy for all of the animals to have chocolate floating around in the water.

There were dogs rolling around in it and they seemed pretty happy. I bet they really needed baths when they got home, though. I don't think the birds liked the way it tasted, or maybe they couldn't see through it to find any worms to eat.

By now, the whole entire lake was full of chocolate milk. I thought this was great since I would have enough chocolate milk to last forever. I would never have to make it myself. I could just go out to the lake and dip my glass in anytime I wanted.

Our neighbor, Ms. Mary, was outside watering her flowers. She looked really upset and called over to my Dad to ask what was going on. She said, "All of this sugar is going to ruin my prized Azaleas. And, what about my tomato plants? They can't drink milk! What should we do?" He answered back, "I'm not sure, Ms. Mary. This is all so strange! Maybe it won't stay like this for too long."

By now, the **rain** had stopped and there was a big, beautiful rainbow in the sky. It was sparkly, brown, orange, red and yellow. My sister and I were wondering about the end of this rainbow. We wished that we could walk over the top of it and slide down the other side.

Maybe we would land in a chocolate lake with chocolate fishes swimming around! She said, "There must be cookies or cereal at the end of the rainbow to eat with all this milk." I hoped there was a treasure chest full of chocolates shaped liked gold coins.

That's when we noticed that fishes and turtles were trying to get <u>out</u> of the lake near our house. Dad said, "Oh no! The fishes can't breathe milk. They need water to survive!"

Dad said, "I have an idea!" He ran off toward our house. My sister asked, "What's he going to do?" I didn't know, but I was starting to wonder if maybe all this chocolate wasn't so great after all. Soon, Dad came running back with his remote controlled boat.

He put the boat in the lake and turned it on. Then he started steering it so it went around in big circles.

It went faster and faster and faster, until it was like a spoon stirring a huge glass of chocolate milk.

The faster he stirred the lake, the less chocolate you could see. Pretty soon, the lake had turned back into blue water. Dad steered the boat back over to the shore and took it out.

The fish started swimming again and everything seemed pretty normal. Ms. Mary was dancing around spraying her plants with plain water, singing, "rain, rain go away... come again another day!" My sister said, "Dad, you must be the best stirrer in the whole wide world!"

So, there we were, covered with chocolate milk and feeling great. The air still smelled sweet and yummy. It was funny that we were so bored just a little while ago, but it turned out to be an amazing day.

Pretty soon, all of the milk evaporated back up to the sky like nothing had ever happened. It was good that people could see how to drive and swim underwater again. I admit that I was disappointed that I wouldn't be able to dip my glass into our lake to get milk anytime I wanted it. But, I knew that my Dad had done the right thing.

Mom smiled and said, "Guess what time it is!" "What?" my sister and I replied together. She said, "It's straight to the bathtub for both of you!" We were leaving sticky brown tracks everywhere we walked. Mom said, "Thank goodness it doesn't rain chocolate milk everyday! Just look at this mess!"

Later, we were eating our cookies and drinking our milk, when my sister said, "Aww, I wish it would have been strawberry milk instead!" Then Mom said, "But, it would have been even better for you if it was just plain."

The End

Stacy Spriggs is an Environmental Scientist, with a B.A. from Rollins College in Winter Park, Florida. She has worked in the environmental protection field in Florida for over 12 years and has always enjoyed writing. Her past endeavors include working with aquatic life, serving in the United States Navy, and managing rental properties in Charleston, South Carolina. She currently lives with her husband and children in Sarasota, Florida.